WASTE MANAGEMENT: PREVENTION, RECYCLING & CONSERVATION

Managing Our Waste Series

• • • • • • • • • • • • • • • • • • •

Written by Erika Gasper Gombatz, M.A.

GRADES 5 - 8
Reading Levels 3 - 4

Classroom Complete Press
P.O. Box 19729
San Diego, CA 92159
Tel: 1-800-663-3609/ Fax: 1-800-663-3608
Email: service@classroomcompletepress.com

www.classroomcompletepress.com

ISBN-13: 978-1-55319-303-6
ISBN-10: 1-55319-303-2

© 2007

Critical Thinking Skills

Waste Management: Prevention, Recycling & Conservation

Skills For Critical Thinking	Conservation	Reduce & Reuse	Recycling	Composting	Fresh Water Resources	Conserving Fresh Water	Clean Air Resources	Sustainable Living	Hands-on Activities
LEVEL 1 Knowledge									
• List Details/Facts	✓	✓	✓	✓	✓	✓	✓	✓	✓
• Recall Information	✓	✓	✓	✓	✓	✓	✓	✓	
• Match Vocab. to Definitions		✓	✓	✓	✓	✓	✓	✓	
• Define Vocabulary	✓	✓	✓	✓	✓	✓	✓	✓	
• Recognize Validity (T/F)	✓			✓		✓			
LEVEL 2 Comprehension									
• Demonstrate Understanding	✓	✓	✓	✓	✓	✓	✓	✓	✓
• Explain Scientific Causation	✓	✓	✓	✓	✓	✓	✓	✓	
• Rephrasing Vocab. Meaning	✓	✓	✓	✓	✓	✓	✓		
• Describe	✓	✓	✓	✓		✓	✓	✓	✓
• Classify Objects Into Groups	✓	✓	✓	✓		✓		✓	
LEVEL 3 Application									
• Application to Own Life	✓	✓	✓	✓	✓	✓	✓	✓	✓
• Model Scientific Process	✓	✓	✓	✓	✓	✓	✓	✓	
• Organize & Classify Facts	✓	✓	✓	✓	✓	✓	✓	✓	
• Utilize Alternative Research Tools	✓		✓		✓	✓		✓	
LEVEL 4 Analysis									
• Distinguish Meanings	✓	✓	✓	✓	✓	✓	✓		
• Make Inferences	✓	✓	✓	✓	✓	✓	✓	✓	✓
• Draw Conclusions Based on Facts Provided	✓	✓	✓	✓	✓	✓	✓	✓	✓
• Classify Based on Facts Researched			✓			✓		✓	✓
• Sequence Events			✓	✓	✓				
LEVEL 5 Synthesis									
• Compile Research Information			✓	✓	✓	✓	✓	✓	
• Design & Application	✓	✓	✓	✓	✓	✓		✓	✓
• Create & Construct	✓	✓	✓	✓				✓	✓
• Imagine Self in Scientific Role	✓	✓	✓	✓				✓	
LEVEL 6 Evaluation									
• State & Defend an Opinion	✓	✓	✓		✓				
• Evaluate Best Practices	✓	✓		✓	✓	✓	✓	✓	
• Make Recommendations	✓	✓		✓				✓	✓
• Influence Community	✓	✓	✓		✓	✓	✓	✓	✓

Based on Bloom's Taxonomy

Contents

TEACHER GUIDE

STUDENT HANDOUTS

✔ **6 BONUS Activity Pages!** Additional worksheets for your students
✔ **6 BONUS Overhead Transparencies!** For use with your projection system
* Go to our website: **www.classroomcompletepress.com/bonus**
* Enter item CC5765 – Waste Management: Prevention, Recycling & Conservation
* Enter pass code CCCC5765D for Activity Pages. CCCC5765A for Overheads.

FREE!

Assessment Rubric

· · · · · · · · · · · · · · · · ·

Waste Management: Prevention, Recycling & Conservation

Student's Name: _____   Assignment: _____   Level: _____

	Level 1	Level 2	Level 3	Level 4
Understanding Concepts	Demonstrates a limited understanding of concepts. Requires Teacher intervention.	Demonstrates a basic understanding of concepts. Requires little teacher intervention.	Demonstrates a good understanding of concepts. Requires no teacher intervention.	Demonstrates a thorough understanding of concepts. Requires no teacher intervention.
Analysis & Application of Key Concepts	Limited application and interpretation in activity responses	Basic application and interpretation in activity responses	Good application and interpretation in activity responses	Strong application and interpretation in activity responses
Creativity & Imagination	Limited creativity and imagination applied in projects and activities	Some creativity and imagination applied in projects and activities	Satisfactory level of creativity and imagination applied in projects and activities	Beyond expected creativity and imagination applied in projects and activities

STRENGTHS:

WEAKNESSES:

NEXT STEPS:

Teacher Guide

Our resource has been created for ease of use by both TEACHERS and STUDENTS alike.

Introduction

This resource provides ready-to-use information and activities for remedial students in grades five to eight. Written to grade and using simplified language and vocabulary, social studies concepts are presented in a way that makes them more accessible to students and easier to understand. Comprised of reading passages, student activities and overhead transparencies, our resource can be used effectively for whole-class, small group and independent work.

How Is Our Resource Organized?

STUDENT HANDOUTS

Reading passages and **activities** (in the form of reproducible worksheets) make up the majority of our resource. The reading passages present important grade-appropriate information and concepts related to the topic. Embedded in each passage are one or more questions that ensure students understand what they have read.

For each reading passage there are BEFORE YOU READ activities and AFTER YOU READ activities.

- **The BEFORE YOU READ activities prepare students for reading by setting a purpose for reading.** They stimulate background knowledge and experience, and guide students to make connections between what they know and what they will learn. Important concepts and vocabulary are also presented.

- **The AFTER YOU READ activities check students' comprehension** of the concepts presented in the reading passage and extend their learning. Students are asked to give thoughtful consideration of the reading passage through creative and evaluative short-answer questions, research, and extension activities.

Hands-On Activities are included to further develop students' thinking skills and understanding of the concepts. The **Assessment Rubric** (*page 4*) is a useful tool for evaluating students' responses to many of the activities in our resource. The **Comprehension Quiz** (*page 48*) can be used for either a follow-up review or assessment at the completion of the unit.

PICTURE CUES

Our resource contains three main types of pages, each with a different purpose and use. A Picture Cue at the top of each page shows, at a glance, what the page is for.

Teacher Guide
- Information and tools for the teacher

Student Handouts
- Reproducible worksheets and activities

Easy Marking™ Answer Key
- Answers for student activities

EASY MARKING™ ANSWER KEY

Marking students' worksheets is fast and easy with this **Answer Key**. Answers are listed in columns – just line up the column with its corresponding worksheet, as shown, and see how every question matches up with its answer!

Every question matches up with its answer!

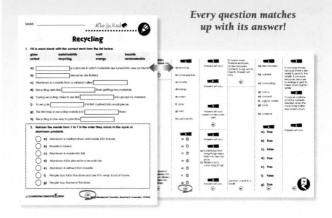

Bloom's Taxonomy

Our resource is an effective tool for any **SOCIAL STUDIES PROGRAM.**

Bloom's Taxonomy* for Reading Comprehension

The activities in our resource engage and build the full range of thinking skills that are essential for students' reading comprehension and understanding of important social studies concepts. Based on the six levels of thinking in Bloom's Taxonomy, and using language at a remedial level, information and questions are given that challenge students to not only recall what they have read, but move beyond this to understand the text and concepts through higher-order thinking. By using higher-order skills of application, analysis, synthesis and evaluation, students become active readers, drawing more meaning from the text, attaining a greater understanding of concepts, and applying and extending their learning in more sophisticated ways.

Our resource, therefore, is an effective tool for any Social Studies program. Whether it is used in whole or in part, or adapted to meet individual student needs, our resource provides teachers with essential information and questions to ask, inspiring students' interest, creativity, and promoting meaningful learning.

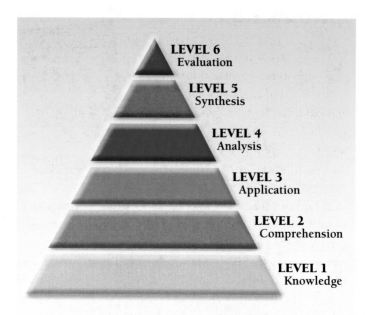

LEVEL 6 Evaluation
LEVEL 5 Synthesis
LEVEL 4 Analysis
LEVEL 3 Application
LEVEL 2 Comprehension
LEVEL 1 Knowledge

BLOOM'S TAXONOMY: 6 LEVELS OF THINKING

*Bloom's Taxonomy is a widely used tool by educators for classifying learning objectives, and is based on the work of Benjamin Bloom.

Vocabulary

conservation	sustainability	recycling	reservoir	renewable
nonrenewable	surroundings	natural resources	petroleum oil	refillable
society	reduce	reuse	plastics	raw materials
packaging	product	aluminum	toxic	hazardous
pollution	pollutant	municipalities	process	chemical
bauxite	nutrients	organic matter	composting	decomposer
facilities	landfills	humus	compost	water purification
sewage treatment	ground water	parasites	wastewater	environment
runoff	filter	contaminate	potable	particles
smokestacks	oxygen	smog	acid rain	carbon dioxide
atmosphere	greenhouse gases	ozone	fossil fuels	alternative fuels
nontoxic	rain water	plant products	Green business	solar panels

NAME: _____

Conservation

1. **Imagine that you put one dollar in a savings account every day. What would happen over time if you began spending two dollars from the savings account each day? Explain your reasoning.**

_____

_____

_____

_____

2. Use a dictionary to look up the word **CONSERVATION** and **SUSTAINABILITY**. Write the definitions on the lines below.

    a) The definition of **conservation** is:

    _____

    _____

    b) The definition of **sustainability** is:

    _____

    _____

3. **Complete each sentence with a word from the list. Use a dictionary to help you.**

recycling	reservoir	renewable	nonrenewable	surroundings

    a) The word [_____] means everything around you.

    b) [_____] resources are constantly replaced by nature.

    c) A body of water used to supply people with drinking water is called a
    [_____].

    d) Resources that are not replaced by nature in time for people to use them are called
    [_____].

    e) Melting down metal cans to make other metal products is an example of
    [_____].

NAME: _____

Conservation

What are natural resources?

Take a look at your surroundings. What things do you see around you? Are you inside a building? Maybe you see lights, painted walls, a concrete floor. Perhaps you are sitting at a desk or table. You might have pens, paper, and markers at your desk. Do your surroundings seem different from the natural world? Actually, everything around you was made from materials found in nature. These **natural resources** include plants, metals, rock, soil, and petroleum oil. Fresh water, clean air, and sunlight are other important natural resources that we need in order to survive.

Describe the meaning of the term <u>natural resources</u>. What natural resources do you depend on in your everyday life?

_____

_____

What are some types of natural resources?

Some natural resources are constantly being put back, or replaced, by Earth processes. For example, fresh water collects in streams after each rainfall. If people take water from a stream, the water will be replaced by rainfall.

Natural resources that are constantly replaced are called **renewable**. Trees are renewable because new trees can grow as old ones are cut. Renewable resources also include resources that are not used up. For example, windmills change wind energy to electric energy. Wind is a renewable resource because it is not used up by the windmills. Sunlight is another example of a renewable resource.

Other natural resources are not replaced in time for people to use them. For example, **petroleum oil** was formed from ancient plants by a process that takes millions of years.

Once we use up the supply of petroleum oil on Earth, petroleum oil will no longer be available to us. Natural resources that can be used up are called **nonrenewable**. **Metal ores** are a nonrenewable resource. Like oil, they take millions of years to form.

Conservation

How can we protect natural resources?

Even renewable resources can run out if people use them up too fast. **Sustainability** is the practice of using resources in a way that will allow people to use them long into the future. For example, think of a town that gets water from one **reservoir**. In order to use the reservoir sustainably, people must use the water more slowly than the water is replaced by rainfall. In other words, the amount of water taken out of the reservoir must <u>not</u> be greater than the amount of water going into the reservoir. If the people use the water faster than rainfall can replace it, the reservoir will run out of water.

There are also more creative ways to use materials sustainably. For example, metals are nonrenewable because they take millions of years to form. However, metals from waste materials can be melted and made into new products. Thus, the same metals can be used over and over again. This process is called **recycling**. Recycling allows materials to be used sustainably.

Describe the meaning of the term <u>recycling.</u>

_____

_____

What is conservation?

Conservation is another way to practice sustainability. **Conservation** means using only what you really need. It also means protecting natural resources. Even renewable resources can become unavailable to people if they are polluted. For example, if toxic waste gets into a reservoir, people may not be able to use the water from that reservoir for many years. Also, if people use more water than they really need, the reservoir may be used up faster than it is replaced by rainfall. To conserve water, people use only what they really need. They also work to protect water sources from becoming polluted.

NAME: _____

Conservation

1. On each line, write the letter **R** for RENEWABLE or **N** for NONRENEWABLE to label the resource being described.

_____ **a)** Sunlight used to recharge batteries.

_____ **b)** Water from a river flowing through a dam to make electricity.

_____ **c)** Petroleum oil used to make plastics.

_____ **d)** Coal that is burned to make electricity.

_____ **e)** Aluminum used to make soda cans.

_____ **f)** Trees cut and milled into boards for building homes.

_____ **g)** Wind used to turn windmills that make electricity.

_____ **h)** Copper used to make pipes.

_____ **i)** Uranium ore used in nuclear power plants to make electricity.

2. Circle the word **TRUE** if the statement is TRUE or Circle the word **FALSE** if it is FALSE.

A) Recycling aluminum is one way to use aluminum sustainably.
TRUE   **FALSE**

B) Conserving a nonrenewable resource like petroleum oil can make that resource renewable.
TRUE   **FALSE**

C) Trees are a nonrenewable resource.
TRUE   **FALSE**

D) Plastic water bottles are made from a renewable resource.
True   **False**

E) Renewable resources are replaced by natural Earth processes faster than people can use them up.
TRUE   **FALSE**

F) Petroleum oil is a renewable resource because it will be replaced by natural Earth processes in a few million years
TRUE   **FALSE**

Conservation

3. How would you explain the meaning of **sustainability** to a younger brother or sister? What examples could you use to help a child understand the meaning of sustainability?

_____

_____

_____

4. Explain how **recycling** a nonrenewable resource can make that resource sustainable, even if the amount of that resource on Earth is limited.

_____

_____

Extension & Application

5. **Create a checklist** of ways for teachers and students to practice conservation in your classroom. Begin by **brainstorming** a list of all of the resources that the people in your classroom depend upon to live and to learn. **Make a T-chart** like the one below. Write the resources from your list in the left column. In the right column, brainstorm one or two ways to conserve each resource.

Resources	Ways to conserve

Use your T-chart to come up with a list of **action steps** that people can use to practice conservation in your classroom. Action steps are phrases that use action verbs. They give people information about the actions they can do to solve problems. For example, "Place bottles in the recycle bin" is an action step with the verb "place."

Be sure your list includes:

* At least eight to ten action steps
* At least one action step that will help conserve each resource in your list
* Action steps that can be taken by everyone in your classroom

Write your steps in large letters on a poster board and display them in your classroom.

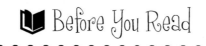
Reduce and Reuse

1. **Imagine that you have a yogurt for lunch. The yogurt comes in a plastic cup with a plastic lid. How could you use the yogurt container again instead of throwing it away?**

_____

_____

2. **Complete each sentence with a word from the list. Use a dictionary to help you.**

conserve	refillable	society	petroleum oil

a) [_____] is a fossil fuel that was made when plants living millions of years ago became buried underneath layers of sediment and rock.

b) A large group of people that share the same culture and institutions is a [_____].

c) One way to [_____] resources is to use only what you need.

d) A juice box is thrown away after the juice is gone, but a thermos is [_____].

3. Fill in the left column with **five** objects that you see around you. In the right column, describe the materials that make up those objects.

Objects	Materials

NAME: _____

Reduce and Reuse

Why is it important to conserve land resources?

What types of materials are used to make buildings, furniture, and school supplies? You might think of metal, wood, plastic, and stone. In order to get these materials, we depend on natural resources from the land.

Rock, metal, and petroleum oil are mined from Earth's crust. Concrete, made of stone and sand, is an important building material. Metal is used in everything from buildings and cars to pens and jewelry. Petroleum oil is used to make plastics. Soil supports the growth of trees, which are used for wood and paper. Our society depends on materials from the land. Therefore, it is very important that we all conserve these resources.

STOP

Describe how society depends upon resources from the land.

_____

_____

What can we do to conserve land resources?

The first step in conservation is to **reduce**, or lessen, the amount of resources you use. What are some ways to reduce? You might first think of not wasting resources, or using only what you really need. You might use both sides of your notebook paper, for example. Another way to reduce is to choose products with less **packaging**. Remember, packaging is made from raw materials, and is simply thrown away when you buy a product.

Another way to conserve resources is to **reuse**. You can often use the same **product** again and again before throwing it away. By doing this, you are saving resources because you end up using fewer products over the long term. One way to reuse is to bring water to school in a refillable water bottle. Many people buy water in plastic bottles that are thrown away after only one use. By using a refillable sports bottle or thermos, you could save many plastic water bottles from becoming waste. Another way to reuse is to save scrap paper, such as worksheets that are printed on only one side. You can use the blank sides of your scrap paper for rough drafts or sketches. What other ways can you think of to reuse products in your everyday life?

Reduce and Reuse

1. Write a list of __ten resources__ that people use from the land.

1) _____

2) _____

3) _____

4) _____

5) _____

6) _____

7) _____

8) _____

9) _____

10) _____

2. a) ~~Cross out~~ the items that are **NOT** reusable.

ceramic cup   light bulb   felt marker   plastic bag   paper napkin

b) (Circle) the materials that are made using stone.

concrete   steel   plastic   pavement   brick

c) __Underline__ the items that were made with resources that depend on soil.

notebook   wooden chair   plastic bottle   paper bag

Reduce and Reuse

3. Explain why it is important for people to **conserve** land resources.

_____

_____

_____

4. Explain **two** ways that you can reduce the amount of land resources you use in your everyday life.

1) _____

_____

2) _____

_____

Extension & Application

5. **Create a display of reusable items.** Set up a table in your classroom to give students and teachers ideas about how to reuse common items.

Step 1: Begin by brainstorming a list of **10 to 12** items that can be reused. Try to think of items that people usually throw away. Take a look in the waste bins at home and school for ideas.

Step 2: Obtain **samples** of each item on your list. Ask your friends, family, and classmates to save the items for you instead of throwing them away.

Step 3: Think of **another use** for each item. Uses can be creative, fun, or practical.

Step 4: Create a display that shows your ideas for how to reuse each item. If possible, set up your items so that people can see how they are being reused. Each item in the display should contain the following:

- a label
- a short written description of its first use
- a short written description of how it can be reused

 NAME: _____

Recycling

---

1. **Do you have a recycling bin at home? Do you have one at school?**
What types of materials do you place in the recycling bins?

_____

_____

---

2. **Complete each sentence with a word from the list. Use a dictionary to help you.**

mixture	chemical	sort	landfill	toxic	fibers

a) A [_____] substance can cause harm to people and wildlife.

b) To [_____] is to place different objects or materials into groups based on their similarities and differences.

c) Two or more different materials placed together in a container is

a [_____].

d) Long, thin strands of plant material are sometimes called [_____].

e) Matter is made from [_____] compounds.

f) A [_____] is a facility where solid waste is buried.

3. **Sort the words below into the three groups in the chart based on the materials that make up the objects.**

can	bottle	foil	cardboard	magazine	sandwich bag

Paper	Plastic	Metal

Recycling

Do you have recycling bins at home and school? Maybe you throw paper, plastic, **aluminum**, and glass into separate bins. Do you know what happens to these materials?

Recycling is different from reusing. When bottles, and cans are recycled, they are not simply washed and refilled. **Recycling** is a process in which materials are sorted, broken down, and brought back to factories where they are turned into new products.

 **Explain how recycling a bottle is different from reusing it.**

_____

_____

Why is it important to recycle?

Nonrenewable resources are limited. Once they are used up, they are no longer available to be made into products. Petroleum oil, metals, and other minerals are nonrenewable. Yet we depend on plastics, aluminum, copper, and steel to make buildings, automobiles, and so many products. One way to keep these materials available far into the future is to recycle them again and again.

Getting **raw materials** can damage the environment. Getting raw materials can also cause pollution that harms people, and can be dangerous for workers. For example, when people mine metals and rock, they often move large amounts of earth. Areas for wildlife can be destroyed. Waste from mining is often toxic and can pollute fresh water sources that people and animals depend on. Finally, mining can be a very dangerous job. Recycling metals causes much less pollution, and is much easier, than mining for new metals.

In many cases, it costs less to recycle materials than to get new ones from nature. This is because recycling often uses less energy than getting raw materials. For example, the aluminum used in cans comes from a mineral called **bauxite**. Making new aluminum cans from recycled aluminum uses only five percent as much electricity as it does to make new cans from bauxite. That is why cash is offered for aluminum cans in many municipalities.

Recycling

How are materials recycled?

During recycling, products must first be sorted by material. Some of the sorting is done by people as they throw away waste. You might separate paper, glass, plastic, and metals in your own home and school. At the landfill or recycling facility, workers further sort the wastes by material.

Each recyclable material goes through a different **process**. Paper is shredded and mixed with water. The mixture is beaten into mush. Then, the water is removed, leaving only the paper fibers. These fibers are heated and pressed with rollers to make new paper.

Glass is crushed into small pieces and melted into liquid. Then, it is molded into new glass containers. Aluminum and other metals are also melted down. Then, they can be formed into new products.

Did you know that most plastics have a number stamped inside of a recycle symbol? This number gives information about what type of **chemical compounds** make up the plastic. It also determines the type of material the plastic can be made into when it is recycled.

STOP

Describe how bottles are recycled.

_____

_____

How can we "close the loop?"

Recycling bottles, cans, and paper is one way to practice sustainability. However, in order for recycling to reduce the amount of resources being used, people must also buy products made from recycled material. When you choose paper made from recycled paper instead of paper made from trees, you are conserving forest resources.

Buying recycled products is often called "closing the loop." The loop, or **product cycle**, begins with raw materials, such as metal. The metal is made into a product that is used, and then recycled. During recycling, the metal is melted down. Then, it is made into a new product. That product can be recycled, and the cycle continues.

NAME: _____

Recycling

1. Fill in each blank with the correct word from the list below.

glass	sustainability	melt	bauxite
sorted	recycling	energy	nonrenewable

a) [_____] is a process in which materials are turned into new products.

b) [_____] resources are limited.

c) Aluminum is made from a mineral called [_____].

d) Recycling uses less [_____] than getting raw materials.

e) During recycling, objects are first [_____] into groups by material.

f) To recycle [_____], it is first crushed into small pieces.

g) The first step in recycling metals is to [_____] them.

h) Recycling is one way to practice [_____].

2. Number the events from **1** to **7** in the order they occur in the cycle of aluminum products.

○ **a)** Aluminum is melted down and made into frames.

○ **b)** Bauxite is mined.

○ **c)** Aluminum is made into foil.

○ **d)** Aluminum foil is placed in a recycle bin.

○ **e)** Aluminum is refined from bauxite.

○ **f)** People buy foil in the store and use it to wrap food at home.

○ **g)** People buy frames in the store.

Recycling

3. Explain how the following materials are recycled

    a) paper: _____

    _____

    b) glass: _____

    _____

    c) metal: _____

    _____

4. Do you think it is important to buy products made with recycled materials? Explain your reasoning.

_____

_____

_____

Extension & Application

5. Learn more about plastics recycling. Research the meaning of the **plastics recycling number system**. You may use the Internet or library resources. Be sure to find out:

- the difference between each type of plastic
- the way in which each type of plastic is recycled
- examples of each type of plastic
- the products that each type of plastic are made into when they are recycled

Create a poster to display the information you learned. Cut out photographs of different plastic products from each group. Write labels for each group to describe the type of plastic, how it is recycled, and what it is made into.

NAME: _____

Composting

1. **Imagine that you left a banana peel outside. What do you think would happen to it? What would it look like after a month?**

_____

_____

_____

2. **Use a dictionary to look up the terms NUTRIENT and ORGANIC MATTER. Write the definitions on the lines below.**

   a) The definition of **nutrient** is: _____

   _____

   _____

   b) The definition of **organic matter** is: _____

   _____

   _____

3. Think of five things that you threw away in the past day or two that were **organic matter**. Describe those things on the lines below.

   1) _____

   2) _____

   3) _____

   4) _____

   5) _____

Composting

Do you recycle all of your paper, metal, and plastic items? If so, food scraps probably make up a large part of your trash. Food scraps can go to a landfill. However, they don't really need to. Food scraps are made from once-living things, or **organic matter**. Organic matter breaks down in nature without any help from people. **Composting** is a way to allow waste organic matter to break down. Broken down organic matter is called **compost**.

In natural environments, like forests and grasslands, living things called **decomposers** break down dead plant and animal matter. Decomposers include bacteria, fungi, worms, and insects. As organic matter is broken down, it releases **nutrients** that plants can use. In nature, compost, or **humus**, forms an important part of soil.

> **STOP**
>
> **Describe the meaning of the word "decompose". Name two kinds of decomposers.**
>
> _____
>
> _____

What are some ways of composting?

Usually, the goal of composting is to break down organic waste materials faster than it would happen in nature. Composting often uses high heat in order to kill plant diseases and weeds in the compost.

You might be surprised to find out that most of your organic matter can be composted at home. If you have a yard, you can start a compost pile. Composting can also be done indoors in special containers. These indoor containers contain earthworms that quickly eat through fruit and vegetable scraps.

In some areas, waste management workers collect organic matter at the curb, along with regular trash pick-up. They bring the organic matter to **municipal composting facilities**. At these facilities, the organic matter is sorted. Woody materials, such as tree trimmings, are shredded and used for **mulch**. Food scraps are placed in very large piles. The conditions in these piles are kept favorable for decomposers so that the food can be broken down quickly.

NAME: _____

Composting

How does composting help the environment?

Composting helps conserve resources. A lot of energy is used to run landfills. By composting, people can send less organic matter to landfills. Composting breaks down organic matter without any added energy.

Composting also helps conserve soil. Compost, or humus, is an important part of soil. It contains most of the nutrients in soil, and keeps the soil light and airy. Plants must take in nutrients in order to grow. Insects and plant roots must have air spaces in soil in order to survive.

You may have learned that nutrients cycle through the environment. Nutrients that are taken in by plant roots pass to animals that eat those plants. Then, to animals that eat other animals. In nature, nutrients are returned to the soil when dead plants and animals are broken down by decomposers. But, if we place our food scraps in a landfill, the nutrients are taken out of the food chain. They are no longer available to plants. However, if we compost our scraps and use the compost to grow plants in a garden, we once again return those nutrients to the food chain.

STOP

Describe how composting helps conserve energy.

_____

_____

How does composting save money?

Composting also saves money. Landfills cost money to operate. Money is needed to buy machines and pay workers. Waste management companies usually charge people for the amount of waste they pick up at homes and bring to a landfill. If you compost food scraps and trimmings from your yard, you can save money by reducing the amount of waste you send to the landfill.

Large companies and institutions can often save a lot of money by composting waste. Grocery store chains, restaurants, schools, prisons, fairgrounds, and amusement parks are among the groups that compost their organic waste. Many of these groups save tens or even hundreds of thousands of dollars each year by composting.

Composting

1. Use the words in the list to answer the questions.

composting	decomposers	compost	organic matter
nutrients	conserve	cycle	humus

_____ **a)** What type of living things break down dead plant and animal matter in natural environments?

_____ **b)** What substances do plants need to take in through their roots in order to grow?

_____ **c)** What is the name of a process in which people help organic waste break down?

_____ **d)** What is another word for compost?

_____ **e)** What is the end product of composting?

_____ **f)** What is another term for once-living things?

_____ **g)** What is the name of a process that repeats the same steps over and over?

_____ **h)** What do you do when you save resources?

2. Circle the word TRUE if the statement is TRUE or Circle the word FALSE if it is FALSE.

A) Decomposition takes place in natural environments.

   TRUE   FALSE

B) Earthworms help break down food scraps in a compost pile.

   TRUE   FALSE

C) Rock crystals are one example of organic matter.

   TRUE   FALSE

D) Metals can be composted because they come from a natural resource.

   TRUE   FALSE

E) Plant roots take in nutrients from the soil.

   TRUE   FALSE

F) Composting is expensive.

   TRUE   FALSE

G) Composting can add nutrients back into the food chain.

   TRUE   FALSE

Composting

3. Explain how composting can save both **money** and **resources**.

_____

_____

_____

_____

4. Explain why **compost** is good for growing garden plants.

_____

_____

_____

Extension & Application

5. Help your family to begin composting

Step 1: Learn more about composting. Contact your **local waste management company** and ask them if they have any composting programs.

Step 2: Determine whether indoor or outdoor composting would be better for your family. Research specific **composting methods** on the Internet or using your library resources. Be sure to find out:

- How to set up an indoor or outdoor compost pile
- The steps you should take to help food break down quickly in your compost pile
- The equipment you would need for an indoor or outdoor compost pile
- How to care for your compost pile
- Any additions you should make to your compost
- Uses for your finished compost

Step 3: **Estimate** how much money your family might save by composting. Find out how much your family pays for waste removal. Ask your waste management company if people pay less money if they produce less waste. Also figure out how much money you might save by using compost to fertilize your house or garden plants.

Step 4: **Design a brochure** to give your family the information they need to start composting. Be sure to include all of the information from Steps 1 to 3 in your brochure.

NAME: _____

Fresh Water Resources

1. **Think about your daily routine, from the time you get up until the time you go to bed. Describe <u>ten</u> ways that you use fresh water during the day.**

   1) _____

   2) _____

   3) _____

   4) _____

   5) _____

   6) _____

   7) _____

   8) _____

   9) _____

   10) _____

2. **Match word to its definition. You may use a dictionary to help you.**

1	**reservoir**	when pollution or harmful substances get into an environment	A
2	**parasites**	human made substances that can harm humans and other living things	B
3	**pollution**	animals that live on other living things, often causing harm	C
4	**wastewater**	the water from rain storms that washes across land and into streams	D
5	**contaminate**	a natural or human made lake that is used as a source of drinking water for a city or town	E
6	**runoff**	water that goes down the drain	F

NAME: _____

Fresh Water Resources

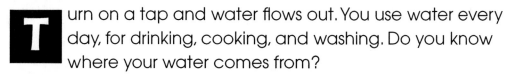

How do we get drinking water?

Turn on a tap and water flows out. You use water every day, for drinking, cooking, and washing. Do you know where your water comes from?

You might have a well that pumps ground water. Or, you might get water from a municipal, or shared, water source, like a stream or reservoir. Most water, especially municipal water, is treated before it gets to your tap. This treatment is called **water purification**. Water purification removes harmful substances in the water that can make people sick. These harmful substances can be natural, such as **parasites**, or from human pollution.

STOP

Describe why water purification is important.

_____

_____

What happens to waste water?

Water from dishwashing, clothes washers, toilets, showers, and tubs, all goes down the drain as waste, or **wastewater**. This wastewater must be treated again before it goes back into the environment. Wastewater from homes contains detergents, food scraps, and human waste. These substances can harm wildlife. Wastewater also includes runoff that goes down storm drains. Runoff contains **pollutants** from city streets. Factories also get rid of wastewater. Factory wastewater can contain all types of harmful chemicals.

Wastewater treatment, also called **sewage treatment**, is an important way to protect the environment. If untreated wastewater gets into streams, lakes, or oceans, it can harm wildlife. It can also contaminate fish that people eat.

Sewage treatment takes place in several steps. Usually, wastewater is first **filtered** to remove larger solids. Then, water is stirred so that air gets into the water. The **oxygen** in the air breaks down many types of harmful substances. Finally, the wastewater is usually passed through another set of smaller filters to remove any additional solids. Then, the water may be released back to the environment.

NAME: _____

Fresh Water Resources

1. Fill in each blank with the correct word from the reading passage.

Where does your water come from? You might get water from a municipal source, like a(n)

_____**a**_____. Before it gets to your house, your water is _____**b**_____.

This Treatment is called water _____**c**_____. Water purification removes

_____**d**_____ substances in water that can make people sick, such as

_____**e**_____ and _____**f**_____. The water that goes down your

drain is called _____**g**_____. It must be treated in order to protect the

_____**h**_____. This process is called _____**i**_____. The first step is to

remove larger _____**j**_____. Then, the water is _____**k**_____ so that

_____**l**_____ gets into the water. The _____**m**_____ in _____**n**_____

breaks down many harmful substances. Then, the water is usually _____**o**_____

again. Then, the water can be released back into the _____**p**_____.

2. Number the events from 1 to 6 in the order they occur in sewage treatment

○ **a)** The water travels into large holding containers where it is stirred so that air can mix with the water.

○ **b)** As you wash your face and brush your teeth, some of the water goes back down the drain.

○ **c)** The water is released back into streams, rivers, a lake, or the ocean.

○ **d)** The water goes through a larger filter to remove some of the larger solid materials, such as tissue.

○ **e)** The water flows through pipes from your house to a sewage treatment facility.

○ **f)** The water passes through a smaller filter to remove any small materials that have not broken down.

Fresh Water Resources

3. Explain why water must be treated both **before** and **after** it goes to your home

_____

_____

_____

_____

_____

4. Describe **three** different sources of wastewater.

1) _____

2) _____

3) _____

Extension & Application

5. Research the **water purification** and **sewage treatment plants** in your area. Work with a group of students. Call your water company or district. Ask them to send you information about the water purification and sewage treatment facilities in your area. Ask them also for information about where your drinking water comes from.

Read through the information from your water company. Write a list of **questions** about things you don't understand, or things you want to learn more about. Use the Internet or library resources to research answers to your questions. Find out more about water purification and sewage treatment methods. Finally, you may want to call your water company to follow up with any unanswered questions.

Design a three-poster flowchart to display in your class. The posters should contain the following information:

- poster 1: the sources of your water
- poster 2: how your water is purified
- poster 3: how your water is treated after it leaves your house

NAME: _____

Conserving Fresh Water

1. Think about what would happen if the water that comes out of your taps at home was no longer available. What would your family do? Where else could you get clean water? How much water would you need? Write your thoughts.

_____

_____

_____

_____

2. Use a dictionary to look up the word POTABLE. Write the definition on the lines below. The definition of **potable** is:

_____

_____

3. Match the word to its definition. You may use a dictionary to help you.

#	Word		Definition	
1	**hazardous**		when harmful substances made by humans get into a natural environment	A
2	**recycle**		substances that can harm living things	B
3	**wetland**		to use materials again for another purpose	C
4	**pesticide**		the place where a plant or animal lives in nature	D
5	**pollution**		an area on the earth that is naturally covered with shallow water, or that floods often	E
6	**habitat**		a substance used to kill insect pests	F

Conserving Fresh Water

How can we conserve water at home?

Fresh water is a very important resource. Although it is renewable, sources of fresh water can run out if people use too much. Sources of fresh water can also become **contaminated** with pollution.

The first step in conserving fresh water is to reduce your water use. Turn off the water when you are brushing teeth. Take shorter showers. Be sure to run clothes and dishwashers only with full loads. Fill gardens with plants that grow well in your area, and that do not need a lot of extra watering.

Another important step in conserving water at home is to be careful about what goes down your drain. Never pour **toxic**, or **hazardous**, substances down your drain or into the sewer. Common household hazardous substances include harsh cleaners, bleach, motor oil, pesticides, and oil-based paints. These substances can contaminate water supplies. Dispose of these substances at a hazardous waste collection site, never down a drain.

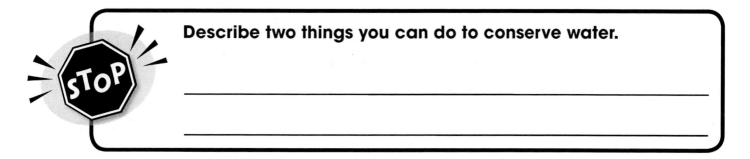

Describe two things you can do to conserve water.

_____

_____

How can cities and towns conserve water?

Cities, towns, and even businesses can use recycled water for some purposes. **Recycled water** usually refers to water that has undergone the sewage treatment process. Instead of releasing the treated water back into the environment, it can be used for purposes other than drinking or washing. Recycled water is often used to water plants along highways and lawns of city buildings. In factories, recycled water can be used to cool machines. Sometimes, towns can even use recycled water to restore wetland

habitats. Recycled water is not for drinking, though. When it is used to water lawns, you might see a sign warning that the water is not **potable**, or drinkable.

Conserving Fresh Water

1. **The list below contains steps to conserve water at home. Fill in the blanks with the missing words.**

   a) _____ the amount of water you use.

   b) Turn off the water when you are _____ your teeth.

   c) Take _____ showers.

   d) Only run the clothes washer with a _____ load.

   e) In your garden, use plants that do not need a lot of extra _____ .

   f) Never pour _____ or _____ substances down your drain.

---

2. **a)** **Circle** the items that you should **NEVER** pour down a drain or sewer.

dish detergent	**toothpaste**	**oil-based paints**
bug spray	**hand soap**	**bleach**
spoiled milk	**motor oil**	**watercolor paints**
soda	**flea powder**	**turpentine**

   b) Explain how you should **dispose** of the items that you circled in the list above.

   _____

   _____

   _____

Conserving Fresh Water

3. What is recycled water?

_____

_____

_____

4. Describe <u>three</u> different uses of recycled water.

1) _____

_____

2) _____

_____

3) _____

_____

Extension & Application

5. Learn more about recycled water. Begin by researching recycled water using the Internet or library resources. Find the answers to the following questions:

- How is water recycled by cities? What facilities are needed?
- How can water be recycled in a home or building? What equipment is needed?
- What are more uses of recycled water?

Then, contact your **local government agencies** to find out if water is being recycled in your area. Find the numbers for your local government in the phone book. Look for the planning department, department of works, environmental departments, or parks departments. Ask the following questions:

- Does our town recycle water?
- Where are the water recycling facilities?
- How is the recycled water used?

Present your findings to your class in a poster or oral presentation.

NAME: _____

Clean Air Resources

1. How do people depend on air? What would happen if the air became too dirty to breathe? Write your ideas.

_____

_____

_____

_____

2. Use a dictionary to look up the word ATMOSPHERE. Write the definition on the lines below. The definition of <u>atmosphere</u> is:

_____

_____

3. Complete each sentence with a word from the list. Use a dictionary to help you.

gasoline   waste   disease   gas   acid   greenhouse   particles

a) [_____] gases can trap heat in the atmosphere.

b) A(n) [_____] is a substance that does not have a definite shape or volume.

c) If your body is not working properly and you feel sick, you might have a [_____].

d) Parts of a substance that are not used are [_____].

e) Tiny pieces of solid substances are called [_____].

f) [_____] is a type of fossil fuel that is used to power automobiles.

g) A(n) [_____] is a substance that tastes sour and can cause some materials to break down quickly.

NAME: _____

Clean Air Resources

How does waste affect the air?

Along with fresh water, people must have clean air in order to live. In that sense, clean air is a resource. We can't use up the air. There is enough air for everyone to use. However, our waste products can pollute the air. Breathing polluted air can harm people's health. In fact, thousands of people die each year from air pollution.

Pollutants enter the air from many sources. Burning **fossil fuels**, such as gasoline and oil, is a major source of air pollution. When gasoline is burned in an automobile engine, waste comes out of the tailpipe. When coal and oil are burned in power plants, waste comes out of **smokestacks**. Waste from fossil fuel burning includes:

- tiny **particles** that can harm lung tissue
- toxic chemicals, such as benzene, that can cause disease
- gases like ozone that can cause **smog**
- acids, such as sulfur, that can cause **acid rain**
- **greenhouse gases**, such as carbon dioxide, that can trap heat in the atmosphere

STOP

Why is air pollution a problem?

_____

_____

How can we protect the air?

Air flows easily from place to place. If pollutants enter the air in one location, they can easily harm people far away. Cities, states, and nations pass laws that help keep pollutants from contaminating the air. In most places, people must bring cars for a regular check-up to be sure the amount of pollutants coming out of the tailpipe is below a certain level. Laws also make factories have scrubbers in smokestacks to remove certain pollutants. You can help protect the air by reducing the amount of fossil fuels you use. Choose to walk or use public transportation, and conserve electricity at home.

Clean Air Resources

1. Match the <u>cause</u> on the left to the <u>effect</u> on the right.

1	**Tiny particles in the air**	can cause disease.	A
2	**Toxic chemicals**	can trap heat in the atmosphere.	B
3	**Ozone**	can harm lung tissue.	C
4	**Greenhouse gases**	causes pollutants to be released into the air.	D
5	**Sulfur in the air**	can cause smog.	E
6	**Burning fossil fuels**	can lessen the amount of pollutants in the air.	F
7	**Smokestack scrubbers**	can cause acid rain.	G

2. Circle the word **TRUE** if the statement is TRUE **or** Circle the word **FALSE** if it is FALSE.

A) Certain laws govern how much pollution can come from the tailpipe of a car.

    TRUE   **FALSE**

B) Benzene is a toxic chemical that can cause disease.

    TRUE   **FALSE**

C) Greenhouse gases are tiny particles of solid material that can cause damage to lung tissue.

    TRUE   **FALSE**

D) Ozone can cause acid rain.

    TRUE   **FALSE**

E) People must have clean air in order to live.

    TRUE   **FALSE**

F) Scrubbers are placed in factory smokestacks in order to take greenhouse gases out of the smoke.

    TRUE   **FALSE**

G) If pollution enters the air in one area, it can harm people far away.

    TRUE   **FALSE**

Clean Air Resources

3. Explain how **air pollution** can harm your health.

_____

_____

_____

4. Describe **two** ways that laws can help lessen the amount of pollution in the air

1) _____

_____

2) _____

5. Describe **two** things you can do to help lessen the amount of pollution in the air.

1) _____

_____

2) _____

_____

Extension & Application

6. Learn more about the **effects of greenhouse gases**. Use the Internet or library resources to find as much information as you can about greenhouse gases. Consider these questions as you do your research:

- **What is the greenhouse effect?**
- **Which gases have the greatest greenhouse effect?**
- **How have the amount of greenhouse gases in our atmosphere changed over time?**
- **What is global warming?**
- **How can global warming affect societies?**
- **How can people work to lessen the amount of greenhouse gases in the atmosphere?**

Prepare a report with words and pictures to share with your classmates.

Sustainable Living

1. Have you ever heard of the terms "Green building" or "Green business"? What do you think the word "Green" means in these terms?

_____

_____

_____

2. Fossil fuels are burned to make electricity. Think about all of the ways you use electricity in your home. On the lines below, write **seven** things in your home that use electricity.

1) _____

2) _____

3) _____

4) _____

5) _____

6) _____

7) _____

3. a) Use a dictionary to look up the word ALTERNATIVE. Write the definition on the lines below.

The definition of **alternative** is:

_____

_____

b) What do you think is the meaning of the term "alternative fuel?"

_____

_____

Sustainable Living

What are sustainable buildings?

Some people choose to use **sustainability** as a goal in designing buildings and running households. The goal of sustainable living is to use as few resources and produce as little waste as possible. Sustainable buildings, also called green buildings, are designed with these goals in mind. Green buildings often use:

- sources of electricity that do not use fossil fuel burning
- building materials that are **nontoxic**
- systems to catch rainwater and use it for watering gardens
- recycled materials

STOP

Describe the goal of sustainable living.

_____

_____

What are sustainable businesses?

Businesses can also practice sustainability. Laws require most businesses to take some steps to conserve resources. For example, factories are not allowed to dump toxic waste into the environment. However, some business leaders are choosing to run their businesses with the model of sustainability.

For some businesses, sustainability means recycling all materials and creating as little waste as possible. Some businesses choose to run stores and factories using renewable energy sources like solar and wind power. Businesses that transport goods can practice sustainability by choosing to run their trucks on alternative fuels. **Alternative fuels** do not use fossil fuels, so they create less pollution. They are often made from plant products, and so are renewable.

Sustainable businesses are sometimes called "Green" businesses. More and more, business leaders are discovering that going "Green" can save them money as well as conserve resources for the future and protect the environment. When you choose to buy products or services from a Green business, you are also helping save resources and the environment.

NAME: _____

Sustainable Living

1. Use the words in the list to answer the questions.

rainwater	nontoxic	wind	fossil fuels
alternative fuels	Green business	plant products	

_____ **a)** Which source of energy causes air pollution when burned?

_____ **b)** What is another term for a sustainable business?

_____ **c)** What can sustainable businesses use to power trucks instead of gasoline?

_____ **d)** What can sustainable homes catch to use for watering gardens?

_____ **e)** Which type of building materials do not have substances that harm people or other living things?

_____ **f)** Which source of power is renewable?

_____ **g)** What can be used to make alternative fuels to power automobiles?

2. Circle the sources of electricity that a sustainable business might use to power their stores.

oil burning furnaces	solar panels	gasoline generators	windmills

3. Underline the goals of sustainable living.

use more petroleum oil	create less waste	recycle more materials
create less pollution	use more fresh water	spend more money

 After You Read

Sustainable Living

4. Explain how using recycled products in a home can help sustainability.

_____

_____

_____

5. Explain why Green buildings and Green businesses look for sources of electricity that do not use fossil fuel burning.

_____

_____

_____

Extension & Application

6. **Create a Green business guide**!

By choosing to buy goods and services from Green businesses, people can help reduce pollution, preserve the environment, and conserve natural resources for the future. Help people in your community choose Green businesses by creating a Green business guide.

Step 1: Search the Internet for Green businesses. Look for businesses that have won environmental awards. Look for national Green business directories. **Keep a list** of the businesses you find. Look for the website address of the business. Then, look in your local phone book to see whether any of the businesses on your list have local stores. Write down their addresses and phone numbers. Check with your local chamber of commerce to find out whether they give Green business awards to small, local businesses, or whether they keep a directory of local Green businesses. Include any of these on your list.

Step 2: Look at how the **business pages** of your phone book are organized by categories. Sort the businesses on your list into similar categories to write your own guide. For each entry in your guide, be sure to include:

• The name of the business
• A description of the services or products they provide
• Contact information, including their website, and a local address and phone number if they have one

When you are finished, ask your teacher for help making copies of the guide to give to students, teachers, family and friends.

Write a Screenplay!

Have you ever watched a movie or television show about people who live in the future? Stories about people who live in the future, or on other planets, are called SCIENCE FICTION. In this activity, you will **write a science fiction screenplay.** A screenplay is a script for a movie or television show. It tells the actors what to say, and includes descriptions of the scenery, or background.

1. Work with a group of **four to five** classmates. Begin by talking about how you think people in the future will use resources. The world's supply of fossil fuels has run out. Answer the following questions:

    *   How do people get energy for their homes and buildings? Do they use electricity? Where does the electricity come from?

    *   Do people still use metals? Plastics? Glass? If so, how do they keep these resources sustainable? If not, what other materials do they use?

    *   What are people's houses like?

    *   Do people still use automobiles? If so, what type of fuel do they run on? If not, how do people get around?

    *   What type of clothes do people wear? What materials are they made from?

    *   Has society solved problems of air and water pollution? If so, how? If not, what is it like to live with the pollution problems?

2. With your group, **brainstorm a general storyline** about people who live in the future. Choose characters for each member of the group. Find a way to work the answers to the above questions into your storyline.

3. **Write your screenplay.** Look in your library for other screenplays. Look through a few samples of other screenplays to get an idea of how they are written.

4. **Practice your play.** You will need a few rehearsals to memorize your lines. Work together to create scenery for your movie. Be creative and have fun!

5. Ask a parent or teacher to help you record your screenplay with a video camera. Edit the movie and show it to your classmates.

Reuse Contest

Hold a contest at your school to find the most USEFUL and CREATIVE ways to reuse everyday items. Work with a small group to run a contest for your class, or work with your whole class to run a contest for your school.

Part A

Create posters to **advertise** the contest. Be sure your posters answer the following questions:

- **Why** should students enter the contest? Tell students why it is important to reuse items instead of throwing them away.

- **What** are the contest rules? What are the prizes?

- **Where** is the contest located? Where should students drop off entries?

- **When** will the entries be judged? When is the deadline for entering?

- **Who** will judge the entries? Who is allowed to enter?

- **How** will the entries be judged? What are the judges looking for? Is there more than one category of winners? For example, you may want to offer one prize for the most practical reuse, and another for the most creative.

Part B

Collect all of the entries. Write a judging checklist that all of the judges can use. To write your checklist, think about what are the most important things you want to look for in entries. Do you want to use a point system for judging?

Part C

Choose the winners and runners-up. Keep the best projects on display for a week or two for parents, teachers, and students to view.

Recycling Audit

An audit is like a check-up. It is a way to make sure everything is going the way it should be. For a recycling audit, you will check around your school to make sure everything that should be recycled is getting recycled.

1

Research the things that can be recycled in your area. Call your local waste management company and find out what things people can recycle. Ask if they have special recycling services for large groups, such as schools. Talk to your assistant principal or operations manager about what recycling programs are in place at your school. Be sure to ask about:

- Recycling paper, cardboard, and magazines

- Recycling metals—which ones are collected?

- Recycling plastics—what numbers are collected?

- How hazardous wastes are handled, and whether they have to be dropped off at a special site

- Whether programs are in place for composting organic matter such as food scraps and yard waste

2

Based on the information you learn, **write a checklist** for your audit. The checklist should contain a list of all of the recycling practices in each room (classrooms, lunch room, library, offices, etc). Which recycling bins are supposed to be placed in each room? Are they being used properly? Are there instructions on exactly what to place in each bin? Are there signs reminding people what to do with their hazardous or organic waste?

3

Conduct your audit. Be sure to use your checklist and check each room in the school. Once you have all of your checklists, analyze the results. What is being done well? What is being done poorly, or not at all? What trends have you observed?

4

Publish your results. Write a brief, one- to two-page report to hand out to all of the staff, and to post in each of the classrooms. In your report, include the answers to the above questions, as well as **_recommendations_** as to how your school community can improve in recycling.

Classroom Composting

For this activity you will **set up a system for composting** food scraps and other organic matter in your classroom. (Be sure to get your teacher's permission first.) If your class has outdoor space or a vegetable garden, you might choose to set up an outdoor compost pile. Otherwise, you can choose an indoor composting system, such as a worm bin.

Part A

Research your composting system. You may use Internet or library sources to find out more about how to compost. Call your local waste management company or local government's environmental department to ask if they offer composting programs or information.

If you want to do an OUTDOOR compost pile, find out the following information:

- What is the best place to put a compost pile? How much room does it need? How far away from structures should it be? Should it be in a covered area or out in the open? Should it be in the sun or shade?
- How should you begin your pile? Will you need to dig a hole, or cover the ground with anything?
- What is the importance of air in your compost pile? What is the importance of heat? How do you maintain the right amount of heat and air in your pile?
- What types of organic matter can be put in your pile? How should you layer the different types of organic matter?
- Should you add anything to your compost pile? What do you need to do to maintain your pile?

If you want to do an INDOOR compost pile, find out the following information:

- What is a **worm bin**, and where can you get one?
- How do you begin composting in a worm bin? What do you need to add?
- What types of organic matter can be put in your worm bin? How much material can your worm bin handle?
- What do you need to do to maintain your worm bin?

Also find out how to know when your compost is finished, and what you can do with it.

Part B

Set up your compost system. Give a presentation to the class to introduce your system and explain how to use it. Be sure everyone understands what they may and may not place in it. Set up a task chart for any maintenance tasks that must be done over time. **Have fun composting!**

CHALLENGE! As your system gets going, why not help other classes begin their own?

NAME: _____

Crossword Puzzle!

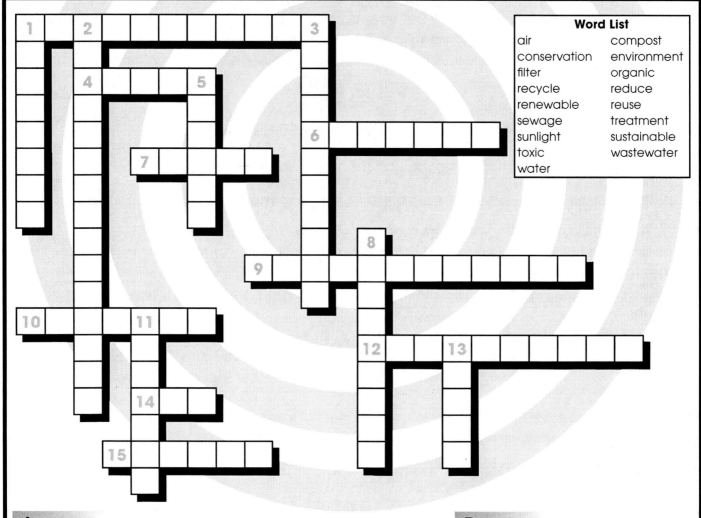

Word List

air	compost
conservation	environment
filter	organic
recycle	reduce
renewable	reuse
sewage	treatment
sunlight	sustainable
toxic	wastewater
water	

Across

1. recycling makes a resource _____
4. an important resource for drinking and washing _____
6. to turn a material from an old product into a new product _____
7. what you do when you refill a water bottle _____
9. the practice of saving and protecting natural resources _____
10. broken down organic matter _____
12. the water that flows down the drain _____
14. the gases in the atmosphere _____
15. how solids are taken out of wastewater _____

Down

1. a renewable resource that can power a home _____
2. what happens to wastewater _____
3. everything that surrounds you _____
5. to use less _____
8. a resource that is quickly replaced by nature _____
11. once-living _____
13. harmful _____

NAME: _____

Word Search

Find all of the words in the Word Search. Words are written horizontally, vertically, diagonally, and some are even written backwards.

aluminum	fuel	nonrenewable	sewer
composting	glass	paper	soil
contaminate	hazardous	petroleum oil	stone
copper	humus	plastic	toxic
decomposers	land	pollution	waste
drain	metal	reservoir	windmills
earthworms	natural resources	runoff	

H	A	N	A	T	U	R	A	L	R	E	S	O	U	R	C	E	S
U	A	S	D	F	G	H	J	K	L	Q	W	E	R	T	Y	U	I
M	P	E	T	R	O	L	E	U	M	O	I	L	B	V	C	X	Z
U	C	V	B	N	M	A	L	U	M	I	N	U	M	Q	W	C	E
S	A	D	N	A	L	S	N	D	F	G	H	J	K	L	C	O	H
Z	X	C	V	B	N	M	O	L	Z	X	W	C	V	E	B	N	N
A	M	F	S	D	R	U	N	O	F	F	A	G	A	H	T	Q
Z	X	E	U	C	P	V	R	B	D	N	N	M	S	R	Q	A	W
A	S	D	T	E	O	F	E	G	E	H	J	K	L	T	Z	M	X
X	C	V	B	A	L	A	N	S	C	D	F	H	G	H	E	I	H
S	O	I	L	S	L	D	E	T	O	Y	V	A	Z	W	F	N	A
Q	W	E	R	T	U	F	W	G	M	U	I	Z	X	O	C	A	C
W	D	F	G	H	T	J	A	K	P	L	Z	A	X	R	C	T	O
Q	I	W	E	R	I	T	B	Y	O	U	Z	R	X	M	C	E	M
X	C	N	V	B	O	N	L	M	S	Q	T	D	W	S	E	R	P
P	X	C	D	V	N	R	E	S	E	R	V	O	I	R	B	N	O
L	A	Q	W	M	E	R	T	Y	R	Z	X	U	X	C	V	B	S
A	Z	P	X	C	I	V	B	S	S	G	D	S	Q	I	W	E	T
S	Q	S	E	A	S	L	Q	W	I	L	A	U	A	U	C	P	I
T	A	D	T	R	D	Z	L	E	U	A	S	I	S	I	Q	O	N
I	S	G	J	O	F	X	H	S	Y	S	D	O	D	P	W	I	G
C	D	A	H	G	N	C	N	R	T	S	F	N	I	A	R	D	S
S	E	W	E	R	Z	E	B	C	O	P	P	E	R	N	E	Y	V

NAME: _____

Comprehension Quiz

28

Part A

8

Circle the word **TRUE** if the statement is TRUE **or** Circle the word **FALSE** if it is FALSE.

A) Nonrenewable resources are replaced by natural Earth processes faster than people can use them up.
TRUE   FALSE

B) Metals, wood, and plastic are all made with resources from the land.
TRUE   FALSE

C) At a recycling facility, plastic bottles are washed and filled with new products.
TRUE   FALSE

D) An apple core is an example of organic matter.
TRUE   FALSE

E) Sewage treatment makes water safe to drink.
TRUE   FALSE

F) Recycled water comes from unopened water bottles that have been sent to a recycling facility.
TRUE   FALSE

G) Automobiles that run on gasoline are a major cause of air pollution.
TRUE   FALSE

H) Green businesses are businesses that try to use as many natural resources as possible.
TRUE   FALSE

Part B

Put a check mark (✓) next to the answer that is most correct.

4

1) Which item could you place on a compost pile?
- ○ **A** plastic bottle
- ○ **B** glass jar
- ○ **C** banana peel
- ○ **D** newspaper

2) Which of these is NOT a use for recycled water?
- ○ **A** drinking
- ○ **B** watering plants
- ○ **C** restoring wetlands
- ○ **D** cooling machines in factories

3) Which substance can cause smog?
- ○ **A** bauxite
- ○ **B** benzene
- ○ **C** carbon
- ○ **D** ozone

4) Which source of energy is nonrenewable?
- ○ **A** solar
- ○ **B** wind
- ○ **C** petroleum oil
- ○ **D** running water

SUBTOTAL: /12

Comprehension Quiz

Part C

Answer the questions in complete sentences.

1. Explain the difference between **renewable** and **nonrenewable** resources. Give examples of each.

⊘ 4

_____

_____

_____

_____

2. Explain how **recycling** is a way to practice sustainability.

⊘ 3

_____

_____

_____

3. What is the difference between **water purification** and **sewage treatment**?

⊘ 3

_____

_____

_____

4. Give examples of how burning fossil fuels harms the environment and human health.

⊘ 3

_____

_____

_____

5. Explain how going "Green" can help a business save money and help the environment.

⊘ 3

_____

_____

_____

SUBTOTAL: /16

1.
Answers will vary

2.
a) toxic

b) sort

c) mixture

d) fibers

e) chemical

f) landfill

3.
a) **Paper:** cardboard, magazine

b) **Plastic:** bottle, sandwich bag

c) **Metal:** can, foil

(16)

1.
Answers will vary

2.
a) light bulb, felt marker, paper napkin

b) concrete, pavement, brick

c) notebook, wooden chair, paper bag

(14)

3.
Land resources are needed to make all of the things we use every day.

4.
Answers will vary

(15)

5.
Answers will vary

1.
Answers will vary

2.
a) petroleum oil

b) society

c) conserve

d) refillable

3.
Answers will vary

(12)

People need resources from the land to make buildings, furniture, and the products that we use in everyday life.

(13)

3.
Answers will vary

4.
Answers will vary

5.
Answers will vary

(11)

Making something new out of materials from old products

(9)

1.
a) R

b) R

c) N

d) N

e) N

f) R

g) R

h) N

i) N

2.
A) TRUE

B) FALSE

C) FALSE

D) FALSE

E) TRUE

F) FALSE

(10)

1.
Answers will vary

2.
a) Saving and protecting natural resources

b) Using natural resources in a way that makes sure they will be available for others to use in the future

3.
a) surroundings

b) renewable

c) reservoir

d) nonrenewable

e) recycling

(7)

Materials from Earth that people depend on to make things and to live. Answers will vary

(8)

25

3. It can save money because there is less waste to send to the landfill. It can save resources because no energy is used to break down organic waste.

4. Compost contains all of the nutrients released when the once-living matter was broken down.

5. Answers will vary

1.
a) decomposers
b) nutrients
c) composting
d) humus
e) compost
f) organic matter
g) cycle
h) conserve

2.
A) TRUE
B) TRUE
C) FALSE
D) FALSE
E) TRUE
F) FALSE
G) TRUE
24

To break down. Possible examples of decomposers: bacteria, fungi, worms, insects. Answers will vary.
22

Less trash is sent to a landfill.
23

---

3. Answers will vary

4. Answers will vary

5. Answers will vary based on resources used
20

1. Answers will vary

2.
a) Substances that living things need to take in to live and grow
b) Material from once-living things

3. Answers will vary
21

1.
a) recycling
b) nonrenewable
c) bauxite
d) energy
e) sorted
f) glass
g) melt
h) sustainability

2.
a) ⑥
b) ①
c) ③
d) ⑤
e) ②
f) ④
g) ⑦
19

They are melted down and made into new products.
17

Bottles are crushed into small pieces and melted down. Melted glass is molded into new containers.
18

3. Water that has undergone the sewage treatment process

4. Answers will vary, but should NOT include drinking or washing

5. Answers will vary

(33)

1.
a) reduce
b) brushing
c) shorter
d) full
e) watering
f) toxic, hazardous

2.
a) oil-based paints, bug spray, bleach, motor oil, flea powder, turpentine
b) Take them to a hazardous waste collection site

(32)

1. Answers will vary

2. Water that is clean enough to drink

3.
1 B
2 C
3 E
4 F
5 A
6 D

(30)

Answers will vary

(31)

3. Water treatment removes substances that can make people sick, such as parasites and pollutants.

4. Water that flows down drains, runoff, water used in factories

5. Answers will vary

(29)

1.
a) reservoir
b) treated
c) purification
d) harmful
e) pollutants / parasites
f) parasites / pollutants
g) wastewater
h) environment
i) sewage treatment
j) solids
k) stirred
l) air
m) oxygen
n) air
o) filtered
p) environment

2.
a) 4
b) 1
c) 6
d) 3
e) 2
f) 5

(28)

1. Answers will vary

2.
1. E
2. C
3. B
4. F
5. A
6. D

(26)

It removes harmful substances before the water gets to people's homes.

(27)

1.

Answers will vary

2.

The layer of gases that surrounds Earth

3.

a) greenhouse

b) gas

c) disease

d) waste

e) particles

f) gasoline

g) acid

(34)

It can harm people's health.

(35)

1.

1 C

2 A

3 E

4 B

5 G

6 D

7 F

2. A) TRUE

B) TRUE

C) FALSE

D) FALSE

E) TRUE

F) FALSE

G) TRUE

(36)

3.

Tiny particles in the air can cause lung damage. Toxic chemicals in the air can cause disease.

4. Answers will vary

5. Answers will vary

6. Answers will vary based on resources used

(37)

1. Answers will vary

2. Answers will vary

3.
a) Different, other than the usual
b) Answers will vary

(38)

To use as few resources and produce as little waste as possible

(39)

1.
a) fossil fuels

b) Green business

c) alternative fuels

d) rainwater

e) nontoxic

f) wind

g) plant products

2. solar panels, windmills

3. create less waste, recycle more materials, create less pollution

(40)

4.

Recycled products do not use new raw materials. They are sustainable because their materials can be recycled again and again.

5.

Fossil fuels are not sustainable because they are nonrenewable. They also create a lot of pollution when burned.

6. Answers will vary

(41)

Answers will vary

(42)

Answers will vary

(43)

Answers will vary

(44)

Answers will vary

(45)

EZ✓

Word Search Answers

Across:
1. sustainable
4. water
6. recycle
7. reuse
9. conservation
10. compost
12. wastewater
14. air
15. filter

Down:
1. sunlight
2. sewage treatment
3. environment
5. reduce
8. renewable
11. organic
13. toxic

Part A

A) FALSE

B) TRUE

C) FALSE

D) TRUE

E) FALSE

F) FALSE

G) TRUE

H) FALSE

Part B

1) C

2) A

3) D

4) C

Part C

1.
Renewable resources are replaced by nature as fast as people use them. Nonrenewable resources are not replaced by nature in time for people to use them. Examples will vary.

2.
Recycling a nonrenewable resource can allow that resource to be used again and again.

3.
Water purification happens before the water gets to your home, and it makes the water safe to drink. Sewage treatment happens after water leaves your home and makes the water safe to return to the environment.

4.
Examples will vary

5.
Green businesses can save money because they do not use as many resources and do not make as much waste. They help the environment for the same reasons.

Publication Listing

• • • • • • • • • • • • • • •

Ask Your Dealer About Our Complete Line

REGULAR EDUCATION

• • • • • • • • • • • • • • • • • •

REMEDIAL EDUCATION

Reading Level 3-4 Grades 5-8

• • • • • • • • • • • • • • •

SCIENCE

ITEM #	TITLE
	ECOLOGY & THE ENVIRONMENT SERIES
CC4500	Ecosystems
CC4501	Classification & Adaptation
CC4502	Cells
CC4503	Ecology & The Environment Big Book
	MATTER & ENERGY SERIES
CC4504	Properties of Matter
CC4505	Atoms, Molecules & Elements
CC4506	Energy
CC4507	The Nature of Matter Big Book
	HUMAN BODY SERIES
CC4516	Cells, Skeletal & Muscular Systems
CC4517	Nervous, Senses & Respiratory Systems
CC4518	Circulatory, Digestive Excretory & Reproductive
CC4519	Human Body Big Book
	FORCE & MOTION SERIES
CC4508	Force
CC4509	Motion
CC4510	Simple Machines
CC4511	Force, Motion & Simple Machines Big Book
	SPACE & BEYOND SERIES
CC4512	Space - Solar Systems
CC4513	Space - Galaxies & The Universe
CC4514	Space - Travel & Technology
CC4515	Space Big Book

ENVIRONMENTAL STUDIES

ITEM #	TITLE
	MANAGING OUR WASTE SERIES
CC5764	Waste: At the Source
CC5765	Prevention, Recycling & Conservation
CC5766	Waste: The Global View
CC5767	Waste Management Big Book
	CLIMATE CHANGE SERIES
CC5769	Global Warming: Causes NEW!
CC5770	Global Warming: Effects NEW!
CC5771	Global Warming: Reduction NEW!
CC5772	Global Warming Big Book NEW!

SOCIAL STUDIES

ITEM #	TITLE
	WORLD CONTINENTS SERIES
CC5750	North America
CC5751	South America
CC5768	The Americas Big Book
CC5752	Europe
CC5753	Africa
CC5754	Asia
CC5755	Australia
CC5756	Antarctica
	NORTH AMERICAN GOVERNMENT SERIES
CC5757	American Government
CC5758	Canadian Government
CC5759	Mexican Government
CC5760	Governments of North America Big Book
	WORLD GOVERNMENT SERIES
CC5761	World Political Leaders
CC5762	World Electoral Processes NEW!
CC5763	Capitalism versus Communism NEW!
CC5777	World Politics Big Book NEW!
	WORLD CONFLICT SERIES
CC5500	American Civil War
CC5501	World War I
CC5502	World War II
CC5503	World Wars I & II Big Book
CC5505	Korean War NEW!
CC5506	Vietnam War NEW!
CC5507	Korean & Vietnam Wars Big Book NEW!

LANGUAGE ARTS

ITEM #	TITLE
	LITERACY SKILL SERIES
CC1106	Reading Response Forms: Grades 1-2 NEW!
CC1107	Reading Response Forms Grades 3-4 NEW!
CC1108	Reading Response Forms Grades 5-6 NEW!
CC1109	Reading Response Forms Big Book NEW!
CC1110	Word Families - Short Vowels: Grades K-1 NEW!
CC1111	Word Families - Long Vowels: Grades K-1 NEW!
CC1112	Word Families Big Book: Grades K-1 NEW!
	LITERATURE KITS GRADES 1-2
CC2100	Curious George (H. A. Rey)
CC2101	Paper Bag Princess (Robert N. Munsch)
CC2102	Stone Soup (Marcia Brown)
CC2103	The Very Hungry Caterpillar (Eric Carle)
CC2104	Where the Wild Things Are (Maurice Sendak)
	LITERATURE KITS GRADES 3-4
CC2300	Babe: The Gallant Pig (Dick King-Smith)
CC2301	Because of Winn-Dixie (Kate DiCamillo)
CC2302	The Tale of Despereaux (Kate DiCamillo)
CC2303	James and the Giant Peach (Roald Dahl)
CC2304	Ramona Quimby, Age 8 (Beverly Cleary)
CC2305	The Mouse and the Motorcycle (Beverly Cleary)
CC2306	Charlotte's Web (E.B. White) NEW!
CC2307	Owls in the Family (Farley Mowat) NEW!
	LITERATURE KITS GRADES 5-6
CC2500	Black Beauty (Anna Sewell)
CC2501	Bridge to Terabithia (Katherine Paterson)
CC2502	Bud, Not Buddy (Christopher Paul Curtis)
CC2503	The Egypt Game (Zilpha Keatley Snyder)
CC2504	The Great Gilly Hopkins (Katherine Paterson)
CC2505	Holes (Louis Sachar)
CC2506	Number the Stars (Lois Lowry)
CC2507	The Sign of the Beaver (E.G. Speare)
CC2508	The Whipping Boy (Sid Fleischman)
CC2509	Island of the Blue Dolphins (Scott O'Dell) NEW!
CC2510	Underground to Canada (Barbara Smucker) NEW!
CC2511	Loser (Jerry Spinelli) NEW!
	LITERATURE KITS GRADES 7-8
CC2700	Cheaper by the Dozen (Frank B. Gilbreth) NEW!
CC2701	The Miracle Worker (William Gibson) NEW!
CC2702	The Red Pony (John Steinbeck) NEW!
CC2703	Treasure Island (Robert Louis Stevenson) NEW!
CC2704	Romeo and Juliet (William Shakespeare) NEW!

VISIT:

www.CLASSROOM COMPLETE PRESS.com

To view sample pages from each book